Mont Orgueil Castle

The castle of Mont Orgueil is built on a rocky promontory overlooking the nearby coast of Normandy. It commands the Royal Bay of Grouville, and has come to symbolise the Island's spirit of independence and distinct identity.

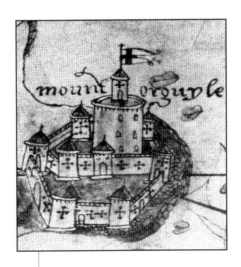

Detail from Poppinjay's Platte, 1563. The earliest known representation of the castle.

Detail from 'A Prospect of Mont Orgueil' by Thomas Philips 1685.

A Souvenir Guide
By Doug Ford

Contents

Looking west from the top of the Keep, over the Royal Bay of Grouville

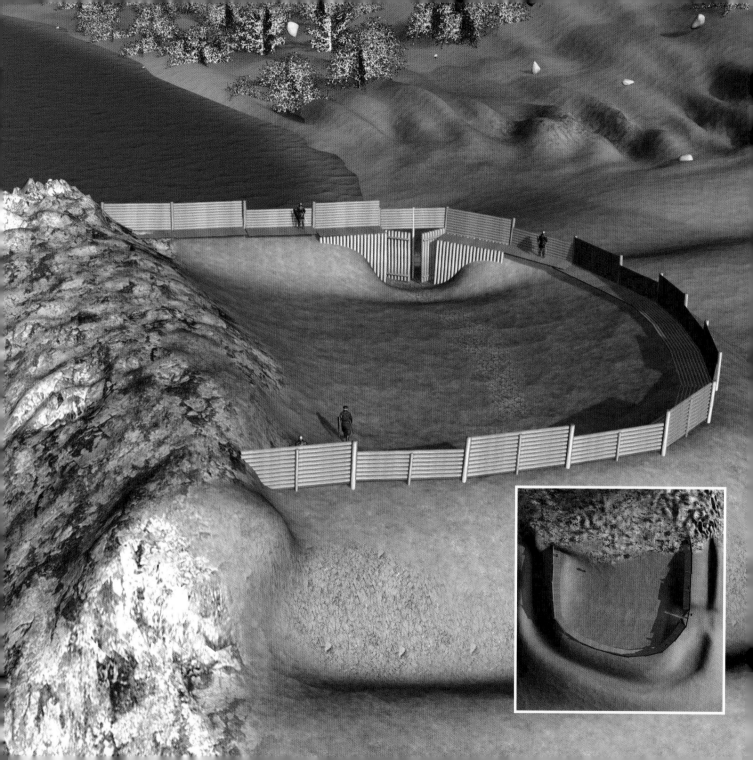

Le Vieux Château

The promontory on which the castle is built was referred to as Gorroic in 1180 by the writer of the Great Roll of the Norman Exchequer. A century later, the Extente of 1274 referred to it as Gorryk. The more familiar name of Gorey first appeared in the 1330s, when French manuscripts referred to the site as Gorri, Gurri and sometimes as Le Château de Gouray. For most of the medieval period the castle was simply referred to as Gorey or the King's Castle – it seems to have acquired the rather more romantic title of Mont Orgueil ('Mount Pride') in the early 15th century, traditionally from Thomas, the Duke of Clarence, a brother of Henry V, although the first written reference dates from the French occupation of the castle in 1462. Once Elizabeth Castle had been built in the 1590s, it was simply referred to as Le Vieux Château.

Before work began on constructing the stone castle it is probable that the old Iron Age hill fort was refortified with a wooden palisade c.1200.

A Castle for the King

Origins

The rocky promontory on which the castle stands is a natural defensive position, protected by steep cliffs and crags and the sea – even the land-approach on to the Castle Green required an enemy to approach uphill.

Archaeological evidence indicates that the advantages of the site were recognised as early as the Neolithic period, about 6,000 years ago. Certainly, by the Iron Age (2,500 years ago) there was some form of defensive structure built on the site. The remains of a ditch and earth ramparts have been identified in the Middle Ward of the castle. Although there is no evidence for its use in the centuries following the collapse of the Roman Empire, it is highly probable that islanders from the east of Jersey would have used it as a place of refuge.

The first Keep c.1212

Jersey became part of the Duchy of Normandy in the 10th century. Until 1204 there was no need for a castle in Jersey; the Channel Islands were a peaceful backwater far from the seat of ducal power. This all ended when the French king, Philip II Augustus, captured Rouen, and Plantagenet rule in Normandy was ended. For two years the Duchy had been split between different groups supporting the French king and the Norman duke, John, who also happened to be King of England and Duke of Aquitaine. In the islands one group took the opportunity to remain loyal to their duke, and so began the Channel Islands' long and peculiar relationship with the Crown of England. The biggest change in the Channel Islands was that

Origins

they were no longer a peaceful backwater and became potential frontier posts on the edge of a war zone. In order to protect the islands, a castle had to be built. Obviously, the place to build it was in St Peter Port, Guernsey, with its deep-water harbour, although when it came to threatening France, the east coast of Jersey was better.

The first documentary sources we have for the castle in Jersey was a letter dated November 1212, in which King John ordered Hasculf de Suligny to hand over the island and the castle to Philip d'Aubigny. Garrisons were sent to both islands and the building programme continued.

A possible reconstruction of the thirteenth century Keep by the Jersey historian Major NVL Rybot

1462 Mont Orgueil . 1499 Montis Superbie . 1515 Chastel de Mountorguyll . 1563 Mount Orguyle . 1595 Mount Orguell . 1606 Mount Orguel . 1610 Mount Orguil

The castle in the thirteenth century

The site chosen in Jersey had been used as a defensive place since the Iron Age and possibly as early as the Neolithic period. The earth rampart and ditch would have been degraded but would have provided a good start for the new fortress which was built on the rocky ridge. The shape of the stone buildings was determined by the narrowness of the ridge, with a hall being connected to two square towers by long passageways. Access to the hall was through an enclosed staircase. The area inside the ramparts below was further strengthened in 1224–5, when 1,000 tree trunks were sent to the islands from the New Forest to make palisades for the two new castles. In addition, Jersey also received five cartloads of lead, the timber from 20 oak trees and 60 bags of nails to assist with the building.

Once built, the castle served as the base for the garrison, which was often recruited from the mainland and maintained by the king's representative, the Keeper, from the Crown revenues. The Close Rolls of Henry III contain many references to arms, shields and coats of mail being shipped to the castle garrison from Southampton and the Tower of London, along with mention of cargoes of timber, beams and lead. There are also numerous entries made by the English Treasury for work and repairs carried out in the castle. The castle acquired a circuit of walls and round towers at this time, and in the 1250s the 'bridge of the King's Castle' is repaired.

1462 Mont Orgueil . 1499 Montis Superbie . 1515 Chastel de Mountorguyll . 1563 Mount Orguyle . 1595 Mount Orguell . 1606 Mount Orguel . 1610 Mount Orguil

As with many castles, work on maintaining fortifications was neglected in times of peace, and so in the summer of 1294 the island was caught unprepared when a French fleet commanded by John d'Harcourt and Matthew de Montmorency mounted a massive raid, laid waste to the island, and according to a petition to the king, over 1,500 islanders were killed. The castle was not taken, although the keeper, Sir Henry de Cobham, does not appear to have taken any real steps to protect the island. The garrison, commanded by Reginald de Carteret, consisted of seven serjeants who had not received any pay, despite the fact that de Cobham had collected the revenues.

In 1327 Sir John des Roches was sent to the Channel Islands to inspect and strengthen defences, and the following year he was appointed keeper. It was probably during his term of office that Grosnez Castle, on the island's northwest corner, was built. At Gorey he strengthened the defences and built a large tower to the north of the Keep, which was to be known as the Rochefort. When he arrived he found the garrison to be made up of three men-at-arms drawing 12d a day, a constable and his attendant drawing 6d a day and 30 foot soldiers drawing 2d. This was obviously a time of international tension because a number of Jersey vessels were attacked by the French and their crews killed, and there had been an attack on Guernsey. In his report to the king, des Roches said that the castle had been partly in ruins, under-equipped and the garrison had not been paid. His report set out a defence plan in which he said that the best way to protect Jersey was for the ordinary defence of the island to be left in the hands of the ordinary people, and the castle to be maintained and manned by an English garrison.

Origins

Detail of men attacking a castle by Rybot

In his accounts, des Roches refers to repairing damage to the buildings in the castle, which had been caused by a great wind. He also describes rebuilding the decaying walls, and names different parts of the castle – the chapel, the pantry, the kitchen, the bakehouse, the prison, houses, turrets and walls. There are also references to roofing the buildings and remaking the bridge. The peacetime garrison is set down as 30 men.

When the Hundred Years War broke out, the island was well protected, the castle being revictualled and garrisoned with archers and other infantry. In 1337 the Constable of the Castle was the Seigneur of Rozel, John de Barentin, who had a garrison of 80 men, which was increased to 94 the following year. He had eight men-at-arms. This was the situation when, on 26th March, Sir Nicholas Béhuchet landed his French army in Jersey. They spent the summer laying waste to the island and besieging the castle, but on 10th September de Barentin was killed whilst leading his men in a sortie. The siege was finally lifted in the late autumn, when the French returned to Normandy before winter settled in. A second expedition was sent to capture Guernsey, which they held until October 1340, when an English expedition led by Walter de Weston recaptured. But the French did hold on to Castle Cornet until 1345.

1462 Mont Orgueil · 1499 Montis Superbie · 1515 Chastel de Mountorguyll · 1563 Mount Orguyle · 1595 Mount Orguell · 1606 Mount Orguel · 1610 Mount Orguil

Betrand du Guesclin and
men attack Mont Orgueil
Castle, 1373

In 1339 Sir Robert Bertram, Lord of Briquebec and Marshal of France, who had been granted Guernsey by the French king, arrived to take up his possession, which also included Jersey. Accompanied by Nicolas Hélie and a large number of barons, the French had a fleet of 35 ships from Normandy and 17 Genoese galleys. The new Constable of Mont Orgueil was Sir Reginald de Carteret, who had a garrison of 12 men-at-arms, six armoured men, 136 crossbow men and 117 archers. The island militia had been reorganised in 1337 into companies of thousands, hundreds and twenties by the keeper, Thomas de Ferrers. This militia was obviously effective because the French spent a little time burning and pillaging but left the island by 12th March 1339. Because Castle Cornet was still in the hands of the French, the King continued to maintain a strong garrison in Jersey. An entry for 1341 has the garrison making brattices.

In 1369 a new threat emerged, and so further work was carried out on repairing and consolidating the castle. In 1372 Ivan of Wales mounted a raid on Guernsey. The Keeper of Jersey and Constable of the Castle, Edmund Rose, enlisted 20 men-at-arms and 20 archers to the Jersey garrison. The following year, when he had been replaced by William de Asthorp, the King ordered the sheriffs of Plymouth and Southampton to hold ships in readiness for the transport of soldiers, horses, victuals, supplies and munitions. In late July of 1373 Bertrand du Guesclin attacked the island and laid siege to the castle. He went for the fast approach to siege warfare, and by concentrating his firepower on one part of the castle he managed to breach the Outer Ward walls. The garrison retired to the inner parts of the castle, and rather than carry on with a war of attrition, they negotiated a position whereby if the castle were not relieved by English troops by Michaelmas, in late September, they would surrender to the French. This allowed du Guesclin to return to Brittany, leaving only a small garrison on the island.

Although a relief force from England did save the day, the weakness of the island's defences had been highlighted, and during 1374 and 1375 the French kept raiding the island. Du Guesclin was able to make the islanders pay a ransom each year in order to prevent him unleashing his forces.

Origins

In July 1403 a Breton fleet commanded by Admiral de Penhouet attacked Jersey, and although the castle held out, the island suffered badly. Little is known of the castle in the early 15th century, although traditionally it received the name Mont Orgueil from the Duke of Clarence, brother of Henry V. During the Wars of the Roses, Margaret of Anjou, wife of Henry VI, negotiated with her cousin Pierre de Brézé, Comte de Maulevrier and Grand Sénéschal of Normandy, and it appears that, as part of a secret deal, Margaret gave up the island in return for French aid – Jean de Carbonnel occupied the castle without a fight, so it would appear that the castle was betrayed. It is around this time that the castle began to be adapted to accommodate cannon and many of the older towers were altered to take the new weapons. A document produced in 1462 lists the artillery and the cannon in the castle, but this was of no real account, for on 17th May 1468 Sir Richard Harliston began a siege which lasted until October, when the French garrison surrendered. The castle was not to suffer foreign occupation again until 1940.

Philippe d'Auvergne, Prince de Bouillon (1754-1816)

In the late 15th century the castle began a transformation into an artillery fortress, which during the 16th century saw work on a massive scale in which the builders were continually being outpaced by the development of artillery. The decision was taken to build a new fortress, Elizabeth Castle, in St Aubin's Bay, which was specifically designed as an artillery base, and Mont Orgueil, the King's Castle, was relegated to Le Vieux Château – 'the Old Castle'. During the 17th century it was used as a political prison for enemies of both Crown and Parliament, and in the 1790s it was the base of La Correspondance, a French anti-Revolutionary spy network headed by Philippe d'Auvergne. The castle ceased to be a military base in 1907, when it was given to the people of Jersey by the Crown for use as an historic monument.

Charles II visited Mont Orgueil in 1646 when he was Prince of Wales and once again in 1649 (by which time he had been proclaimed king in Jersey)

Origins

clockwise from above:
The new artillery arrangement
of the Rampier and New Mount,
the castle *c*.1600, the castle
under occupation 1945.

When the Germans occupied the island in 1940 they recognised the strength of the position and gradually refortified the site with fire control and observation towers, dug-outs, trenches and several gun positions, while the larger rooms in the Keep were fitted out as barracks. Happily, the castle was never used in anger, and following the Liberation in May 1945 it reverted to its role as a monument and visitor attraction.

Tour of the Castle

The castle is essentially split into four main areas: the Outer Ward, the Lower Ward, the Middle Ward and, sitting on the highest part of the promontory, the Keep. The castle builders' idea was that each of these wards would be dominated by its neighbour.

Three sides of the promontory are washed by the sea, while the fourth is the land approach to the castle – the Castle Green – and the only direction from which a serious assault on the castle could be made. In the 13th century a wooden palisade ran from the Main Gate to the cliff edge. This was intended to delay an attack and force the enemy into a position where they could be struck by a concentrated hail of arrows. Behind this palisade a dry ditch, crossed by a drawbridge, created another obstacle to the attackers.

Today's visitors can also approach the castle from the pier via a Water Battery built in 1801 to take cannon to protect the anchorage, which in turn was built over earlier 17th century remains. The staircase leads up around the base of the 13th century John Hélie Tower, through the Outer Ward garden and into the castle.

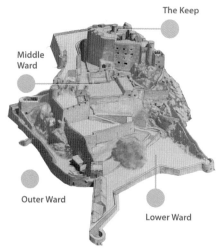

The Keep

Middle Ward

Outer Ward

Lower Ward

Above left The castle from Mont St Nicolas
Left The castle from the Water Battery

The exhibition . . . .

is centred on the Medieval World and the role Jersey played in it. Unlike most venues, there is no real, single space large enough within the castle to house an exhibition, and so the exhibits are all stand-alone displays and are scattered throughout the monument. They focus on the different contexts in which the castle can be viewed and are arranged according to the Great Chain of Being. This places geology at the bottom of the journey through the castle, which takes in natural history, social and military history, the 'marvellous', political history and religious history in a hierarchical sequence that would be instantly recognisable to the Medieval mind.

Following discussions between curators and artists, initial ideas were transformed through a process of research, proposals and responses, into artistic responses to different aspects of the castle's role in the island.

Plan of Mont Orgueil Castle

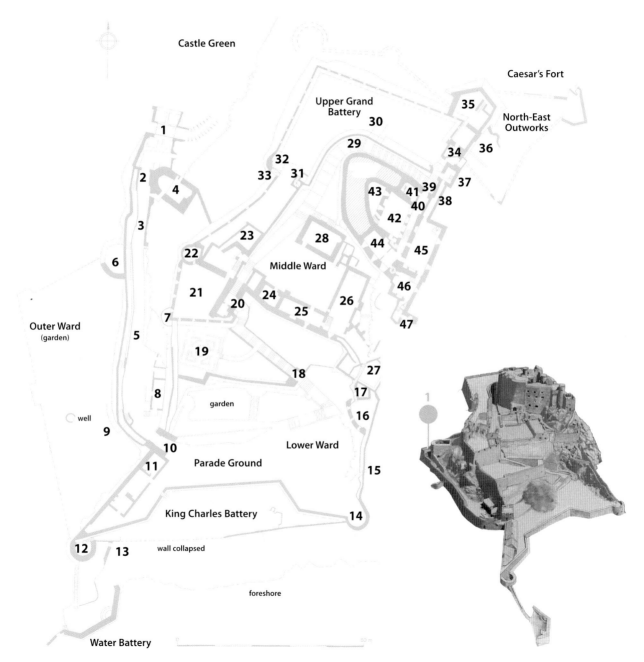

Castle Green

Caesar's Fort

Upper Grand
Battery

North-East
Outworks

35

30

29

34

36

1

32

33 31

2

4

43

41 39

3

40 38

37

42

23

28

44

45

22

Middle Ward

6

46

21

24

26

20

25

47

7

Outer Ward
(garden)

5

19

27

18

17

8

garden

16

well

9

Lower Ward

10

15

11

Parade Ground

King Charles Battery

14

12 13

wall collapsed

foreshore

Water Battery

The Outer Ward

This was originally a large enclosed area, its original western wall running along the length of what is now a row of quayside buildings. The Outer Ward is dominated by the curtain walls and towers enclosing the Lower Ward and the Middle Ward. Should an enemy have managed to enter the castle, and this area had been lost, then the defenders would have withdrawn through the Second Gate to carry on their defence. When the medieval wall collapsed in the 16th century, this area was abandoned and a new wall was built to defend the roadway running between the First and Second Gates. The Crown sold the land for building in 1821 and the community we now refer to as Gorey Pier sprang up.

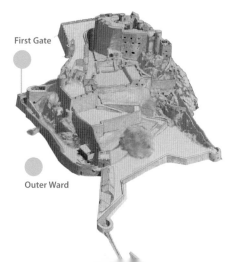

First Gate

Outer Ward

'Seated upon a Rocke, full large and high,
Close by the Sea-shore, next to Normandie,
Neare to a Sandy Bay, where boats doe ride
Withen a Peere, safe both from Wind and Tide.
Three parts thereof the flowing seas surround,
The fourth (North-west-wards) is firme rockie ground…'

The Outer Ward

Entry to the castle was controlled by the defences centred on the First Gate. For many people this was the first point of contact with the island governors, and so the gateway had to be strong and imposing. The outline of the 16th century Gatehouse demolished on the orders of Sir Walter Raleigh in about 1600 can still be seen in the ground in front of the present gate, which was largely rebuilt in the late 18th century. The Harliston Tower, which flanks it, was built in about 1470 and has gun embrasures as well as arrow loops – it was probably the first part of the castle to be purpose-built to take cannon. It remained roofed until the First World War. The small postern gate with the square lintel was built in the 18th century to replace an earlier doorway that was blocked when the area in front of the tower was backfilled. The arch of this blocked doorway can still be seen in the masonry. The tower was named after Sir Richard Harliston, who recaptured the castle from the French in 1468 and ended a seven-year French Occupation of the island.

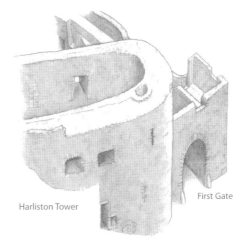

Harliston Tower

First Gate

The remains of the original 13th century main gate are about 20 metres behind the existing gate, where traces of the portcullis slots, the springers of the arched roof and the rear archway can all be seen in the left-hand side wall. This gatehouse was demolished in the 16th century, when the Outer Ward was abandoned and the new wall was built to protect the roadway leading to the Second Gate, while a narrow doorway leads to the Half-Moon Bastion, or Picardy, whose cannon protected the anchorage.

The building in which the modern reception area is housed was erected in 1810 as a Coal Store, then converted into the Stable Store in 1836.

Round towers and curtain walls dominating the roadway

The defended roadway leading to the second gate

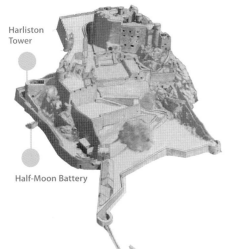

Harliston Tower

Half-Moon Battery

Mystery One – An extended Outer Ward?

The first line of defence against any attack on the castle would have been provided by the walls of the Outer Ward. It seems strange, therefore, that every writer in describing the castle highlights the weakness offered by the exposed north-west corner, which should it be breached would give access straight into the Middle Ward.

With this in mind, it would have been logical for the castle builders to have extended the wall around the north end of the castle to link up with the ridge – however, this can only be conjecture because later modifications to the castle caused by the building of the Grand Battery resulted in the rock face being quarried away and any archaeological evidence would have been lost. The scarcity of written descriptions of the early castle means that there is no surviving historical evidence for an extended Outer Ward – however, it would be the common sense approach to take.

The Second Gate

The next part of the castle, the Lower Ward, was entered through a gate which was approached by a ramp leading to a drawbridge. The counter-balance pit and the axle for this can still be seen beneath the present wooden bridge.

This Second Gate, named the Thynne Gate after Sir John Thynne, in 1549, was originally built in the 13th century as an open-backed tower, although rather than be exposed to the elements it could have had a wooden fourth wall, which could have been removed easily to prevent attackers using it as a strong point should they capture it. In the 15th or early 16th century the stone vaulted ceiling and the fourth wall were added. Throughout the 17th and 18th centuries the chamber over the gate was used as a prison, before a gabled roof was built over the top in 1800 and it became the gunners' quarters. This roof was dismantled in the 1920s.

As part of the reorganisation following the abandonment of the Outer Ward in the late 16th century, a small doorway, the West Postern, was built. Nowadays this leads to the Outer Ward Garden and a path leads down to the Water Battery and the harbour.

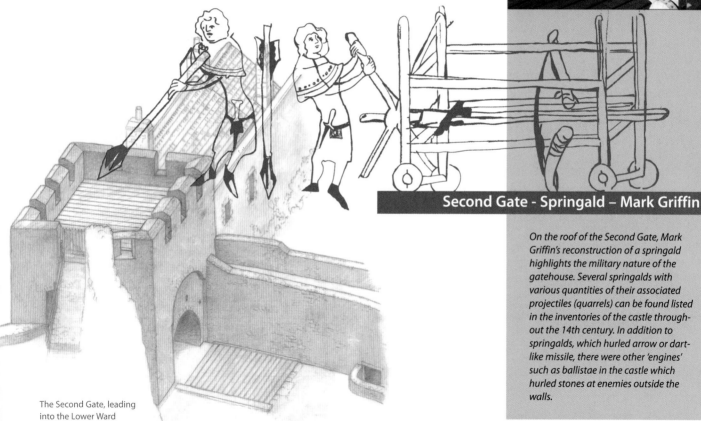

The Second Gate, leading into the Lower Ward

Second Gate - Springald – Mark Griffin

On the roof of the Second Gate, Mark Griffin's reconstruction of a springald highlights the military nature of the gatehouse. Several springalds with various quantities of their associated projectiles (quarrels) can be found listed in the inventories of the castle throughout the 14th century. In addition to springalds, which hurled arrow or dart-like missile, there were other 'engines' such as ballistae in the castle which hurled stones at enemies outside the walls.

The Half-Moon Bastion was built once the Outer Ward was abandoned

Outer Ward - Garden and carved stones – Gordon Young

In the Outer Ward Garden, large, painted letters carved into stone by sculptor Gordon Young describe the various historical spellings of Gorey and Mont Orgueil taken from a variety of sources over the centuries. From Gorroic in 1180 to the appearance of Mont Orgueil in 1462.

Further stones carry verses written by the 17th century politician William Prynne, who was imprisoned here during the years before the English Civil War. These poems represent one of the earliest published books relevant to the Island.

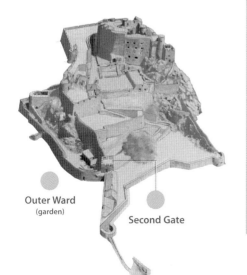

Outer Ward
(garden)

Second Gate

The Lower Ward

Through the Second Gate the second major area of the castle can be found – the Lower Ward. Again, this area is dominated by the original Curtain Walls and the Cross Wall of the Middle Ward, as well as the later de Carteret Rampart and Cornish Bastion. In the Middle Ages there would have been a series of buildings of less permanent nature than the stone walls, and if an enemy threatened to break through they would have been burned to the ground in order to create an open killing ground. Over the years they became more permanent, and eventually a number of administrative buildings were set in this ward – the Courthouse, the Sutler's House and the Viscount's Office. Some of these were still standing as late as 1800, when it was cleared to create the open area known as the Barrack or Parade Ground of the Garrison. The Lodge, which now houses the café, is one of the few surviving relics of the castle's later military role. A plan of the castle in 1680 showed stables on this spot, while the map of 1755 marks it down as the Guard House and Gunners' House. By the end of the eighteenth century it served as the Officers' Quarters, and then by the 1830s it was the Canteen.

Tudor re-enactors in the Lower Ward

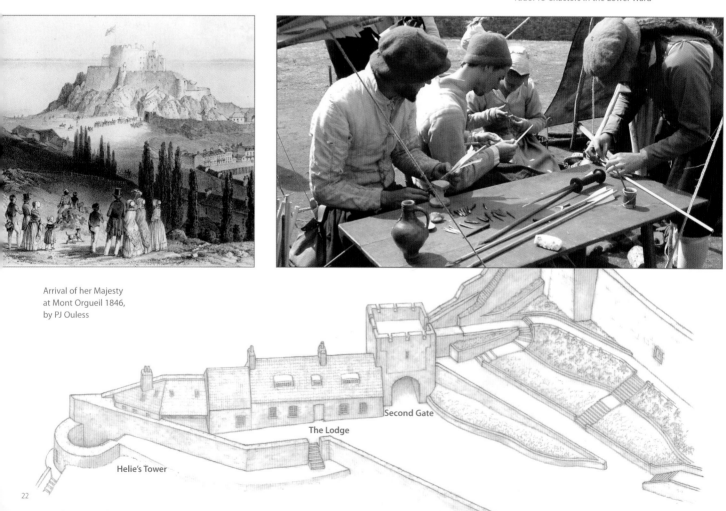

Arrival of her Majesty
at Mont Orgueil 1846,
by PJ Ouless

Second Gate

The Lodge

Helie's Tower

Mont Orgueil from the South, by Heriot

The Lower Ward

The original southern medieval curtain wall ran between the John Hélie Tower and the Southern Tower, and in 1666 a low-level gun platform was built just behind it. This was named the King Charles Battery in honour of Charles II. At the end of the eighteenth century the wall was undermined by the sea and collapsed, and so, in 1801, the remaining section was realigned and reduced in height. The gun position was replaced by a rebuilt Water Battery lower down the slope and by the Parade Battery, which was built on higher ground just behind it. To prevent further erosion, a seawall has been built at the base of the slope.

The John Hélie Tower was originally built in the thirteenth century as a flanking tower, although the first known reference to it is in 1340, when it was described as *Turris ultima versus maris* – 'the last tower before the sea'. It was first associated with John Hélie in 1531. There was a postern gate cut through the medieval wall at this point, and in 1549 the tower was referred to as the Postern Tower. When the Water Battery was built in the seventeenth century to protect the anchorage, a staircase and flanking wall linked it to the tower.

Southern Tower, the sea bench – Chris Bailey

Sculptor Chris Bailey has created a wooden bench to illustrate the marine life to be found in the Royal Bay of Grouville. Each of the four levels of the bench is carved with an image of marine life grouped in 'ascending biological order' – seaweeds, marine worms, molluscs, crustaceans, fish and marine mammals.

At the other end of the Medieval Wall was the Southern Tower, from the top of which ran a passage inside the eastern curtain wall up to the Middle Ward. Mont Orgueil could be threatened from the sea after cannon were successfully mounted on board ships, and so from the middle of the sixteenth century onwards steps were taken to adapt the medieval castle to meet this danger. However, the tower was reduced in height at the end of the eighteenth century when a traversing gun was placed here.

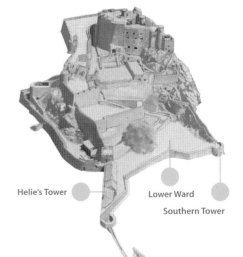

Helie's Tower

Lower Ward

Southern Tower

Southern Postern, plants – Dixie Lee Whiteman

Looking up from the Southern Postern. By using the natural rock outcrops the medieval castle builders were able to create the illusion of lofty walls.

There are over 130 species of plants to be found in the castle and its associated grasslands and rock surfaces. Lichens and bryophytes grow on the natural rock outcrops and the ancient walls. This plant life is important in supporting a range of invertebrates in the castle. Some of these plants, such as the balm-leaved figwort, are at the northernmost limit of their range, and so appear in the British Red Data Book for Nationally Endangered Species. However, they are quite common on the Continent nearby. This question of national scarcity within a UK context also appears with the invertebrates.

The Lower Ward

Next to the Southern Tower a small sally port at the base of the wall gives access to the outside of the castle. When the castle was under siege one man could easily defend it because it was so narrow and access was difficult.

As artillery developed, the castle had to be adapted to meet the demands of a new type of warfare, and the Cornish Bastion was built against the medieval curtain wall in 1547. It takes its name from its builder, Henry Cornish, whose coat of arms can still be seen set into the facade. The bastion controlled the Lower Ward with its three small cannon embrasures, while the three downward-angled gun ports allowed defenders to clear the base of the bastion of any threat, using swivel-mounted guns. It is interesting to note that these have crosslets for crossbows associated with them, while the gun embrasures have musket loops on either side of them. Access to the bastion was from the Middle Ward, via the Prison Tower.

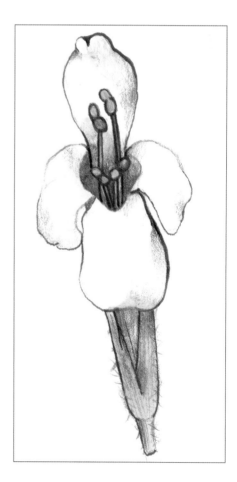

Cornish Bastion with detail of
the Cornish coat of arms

The Lower Ward

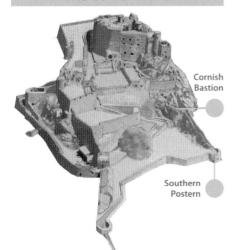

Cornish
Bastion

Southern
Postern

The Lower Ward, lizards – Gordon Young

*In Gordon Young's sculpture the
Common Wall Lizard (Podarcis muralis)
suns itself on a rock. The castle hosts
Britain's largest population of this
species. They grow to be about 15cm
long and live on a diet of insects that
they forage for in the long grass and
among stony outcrops. As reptiles, they
obtain their heat externally, principally
from basking in the sun, while in the cold
months of winter they find refuge in
safe, frost-free holes in walls or in deep
rock crevices. This is why the soft
landscape management scheme used in
the castle is so important in maintaining
their habitat.*

Table, heraldic animals – Chris Bailey

Chris Bailey has created two long picnic tables with shield shapes featuring carvings of the birds that can be seen in and from the castle. These include those species that nest there, such as kestrels ands swifts, those that stop off at the castle as they migrate through the region, such as warblers and firecrests, the seabirds of the bay, such as turnstones and terns, and the flying mammals – the bats.

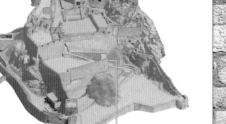

Fourth gate-called the
Queen Elizabeth Gate

The northern end of the Lower Ward originally sloped quite steeply up to the Middle Ward. A staircase led up to the Iron Gate, but this was lost when the de Carteret Rampart was built during the English Civil War in the late 1640s. Sir George Carteret was the leader of the Royalists in Jersey, which he held for the king until 1651. He dropped the 'de' from his name when he was in the Royal Navy in the 1620s and 1630s as he felt it made him sound too French. This new rampart forced an enemy to pass beneath the guns of the Cornish Bastion and allowed cannon to be sited higher up in the Lower Ward, which in turn allowed them to shoot further. It also had the effect of creating a barbican or defended courtyard in front of the newly extended Queen Elizabeth Gate (previously known as the Iron Gate).

The Lower Ward

The de Carteret Gate was a simple two-storey gatehouse built at the same time as the de Carteret Rampart between 1648 and 1650. By being at an angle at the end of the rampart, the gate was protected from direct attack. An interesting feature of the arch is that the two shoulder stones, partly hidden behind buttresses, seem to indicate an earlier date, and so may mean that they have been reused from an earlier gate – possibly the one leading up to the Iron Gate that was lost when the rampart was built.

Although the gatehouse was built in the seventeenth century, it still has many medieval features. The gateposts were held in place at the top by a worked granite stone, and at the bottom by a pintle held in a small hole. The doors were secured by long wooden bars sliding into the bar holes, and the portcullis slots can still be seen on either side. When it was built, the gate was originally a little higher than the wall, but it was reduced in height in the late eighteenth or early nineteenth century. It is occasionally called the Queen's Gate because an inscribed stone was set just above the arch to commemorate Queen Victoria's visit to the castle in 1846.

The coat of arms set in the wall is that of King Charles II. This was originally in the wall of the King Charles Battery, was then set into the new 1801 wall and was finally placed here in 1929.

Left
The de Carteret gate

Above
Queen Victoria's Visit 1846

The 1593 accounts show that Peter Byson (Bisson) was paid 33 shillings, six pence for carving the Royal Arms and setting them in the wall.

In a plan of 1680, the enclosed area created by the de Carteret Rampart was set out as a formal garden, and this has now been recreated. The original thirteenth-century West Curtain Wall ran up the castle rock from the Second Gate to the Middle Ward Cross Wall. At some stage in the late fourteenth or early fifteenth century a structure was built in, and the remains of two windows with window seats, and a fireplace can be still be seen. By the late sixteenth century this was recorded as a two-storey 'ward house before the Iron Gate'. The house and adjoining round tower would have been abandoned and possibly demolished when Paul Ivy extended the Iron Gate in the late sixteenth century.

The Lower Ward

The original entrance into the Middle Ward was through a fortified gate in the Cross Wall, which was originally defended by a simple square tower, which, since the early twentieth century, has been referred to as the St George's Tower. However, this was strengthened in the late thirteenth or early fourteenth century when a long narrow barbican with a machicolated parapet was built onto the front and a gate was set into its west wall, facing the Western Curtain Wall. This created a killing ground, in which anyone attempting to enter the new Iron Gate was overlooked on three sides.

In the early 1590s a new east-facing gateway, protected by a short flanker, was cut into the wall. Above the arch there are three coats of arms carved in stone. Viewed from left to right are the arms of the Paulet family, Queen Elizabeth and Sir Anthony Paulet, which are halved with those of his wife, Katherine Norreys. It is because of these carvings that the gate is called the Queen Elizabeth Gate.

Above
The Fourth Gate from the Prison Tower

Below
The formal garden based upon a plan of 1685

Queen Elizabeth Gate, the Wound Man – Owen Cunningham

Owen Cunningham's sculpture is a three-dimensional representation of the medieval surgical illustration known as the Wound Man. These illustrations show the range of wounds commonly resulting from battle, and feature a human figure whose body is pierced by an assortment of weapons and wounds. In essence, the surgeons were saying 'if you are wounded like this then we can possibly do something for you!' The scale of Owen's work is grossly exaggerated in order to highlight this more violent aspect of the castle's function in the past.

The Lower Ward

The old west-facing gateway was blocked up and the end of the barbican was closed off to create a porter's lodge. The redundant courtyard was then filled in and Paul Ivy's Bulwark was created.

The Inner Gate has been adapted over the centuries. During the 1590s the floor level was cut away by up to as much as 2.6 metres and ten stairs were built. The original ground level would have been about 20 cm below the portcullis slots, which can be seen on either side of the passage. The remains of the bar holes can also still be seen in the walls.

The gatehouse was flanked by guardrooms on either side, which were accessed from the floor above. The visitor can still make out the outline of the blocked inspection windows in the walls. The beginning of the vaulting, which would have supported a first-floor room over the entrance, can still be seen at the top of the remaining wall.

The Middle Ward

The Middle Ward is dominated by the massive bulk of the handiwork of the Tudor governors. It is the third major part of the castle and there is evidence that the area has been occupied for at least 2,000 years, but most of its medieval features were lost in the sixteenth century, when the massive Rampier was constructed and the Keep was extended, and during the seventeenth century, when the surface was levelled.

Immediately to the left of the gate is the doorway leading up to Paul Ivy's Bulwark. Work on this angled flanker tower began in 1593, when the Iron Gate was being remodelled by the Queen's Engineer, Paul Ivy. The parapet and the magazine may have been completed by Sir John Peyton 20 years later. In 1621 it was described as the 'Bulwark over ye Yron Gate', and for most of the twentieth century Sir John Peyton was given the credit for building the whole structure. By the eighteenth century the staircase leading up to the Bulwark was in a dangerous condition and so was blocked off.

The Grand Battery, or Rampier, was built during the second half of the sixteenth century as a response to the increased use of cannon. It wraps around the New Mount, or Somerset Tower, but appears to have been left unfinished. The holes in the wall are known as putlog holes and were used to hold scaffolding or building platforms. When work was completed they could be either closed up or left open (as here), to serve as weep-holes, allowing water to drain out of the fill of the thickened walls.

The unfinished section of the Grand Battery contains some dressed stones in the infill rubble, which would suggest a date in the second half of the sixteenth century, following the Reformation and the demolition of religious houses and chantries in Jersey.

The building of the Grand Battery in the Middle Ward involved realigning the old medieval curtain wall. Anything built against the inside of the walls would have been lost in the infill when the gun platform was put up.

Paul Ivy Bulwark, Playground – Andy Frost

On the Paul Ivy Bulwark, play area designer Andy Frost depicts a variety of medieval building techniques and the technology used in the past, although they are not intended to be a literal description. This aspect of the castle's past is often overlooked as people tend to remember the names of knights rather than those of the builders. The exhibit names a number of medieval craftsmen and lists some of the work they carried out.

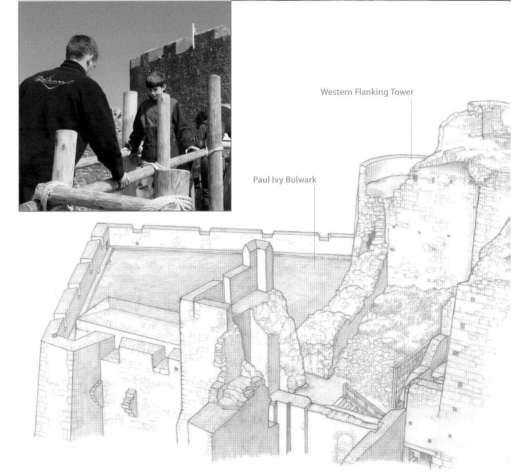

Western Flanking Tower

Paul Ivy Bulwark

The Middle Ward

The ruined square building looking onto the grass was named as the Old Chapel on a plan of 1741, and as the 'Ruins of St George's Chapel' on a 1755 plan; however, for most of the twentieth century it was referred to as the St George's Hall. Archaeological investigations in the 1970s suggested that it was built in the seventeenth century. The entrance was on the ground floor in the south-west corner, while on the first floor there is a doorway in the north-east corner. A fireplace at this level suggests a domestic use. A now ruined staircase behind the east wall, which is associated with the Long Cellar, led up to a larger staircase built against the façade of the Residential Apartments.

Middle Ward, Sir Hugh Calveley – Owen Cunningham

Long Cellar

Old Chapel

Sat astride his charger, Owen Cunningham's magnificent figure of Sir Hugh Calveley (1320–94) portrays the more romantic notion of medieval warfare. The figure is based on the memorial sculpture of Sir Hugh found on his tomb in the church at Bunbury, Cheshire. Calveley was a renowned warrior in his time and was appointed Keeper of the Isles in 1376. The complex nature of fourteenth-century armour is clearly seen in the sculpture. This is the only contemporary image of a medieval soldier who was known to have been at Mont Orgueil.

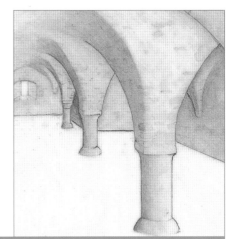

The Long Cellar building is one of the most interesting in the castle. This two-storey building was built in the fourteenth or fifteenth centuries but was a ruin by the eighteenth century. Because the ground floor was vaulted in the manner of a crypt, it became popularly known as the Crypt of the Chapel of St George in the 1830s, and when it was reconstructed in the early twentieth century it was made to look like a thirteenth-century building. In 1915 a medieval altar stone inscribed with five consecration crosses representing the Five Wounds of Christ was placed in the northern end of the cellar. This was one of several found around the castle, where they had been used as builder's infill in the years following the Reformation. It is possible that the building has always had a domestic rather than a religious purpose.

The two blocked-up windows behind the altar show that the building was originally freestanding, while the two larger windows in the southern end of the Cellar cut through the medieval cross wall and were probably gun positions overlooking the Lower Ward – predating the Cornish Bastion by at least 50 years. (One of the windows is in the walled-off area in the south-west corner, which may have been built to take a staircase leading to the first-floor chambers.)

The low wall running parallel to the building is all that remains of a corridor that led to a two-storey building put up against the Cross Wall in the seventeenth century. The larger of the two rooms has been described as an Undercroft, while above it was a Barracks. In the early 1970s a short stretch of Iron Age rampart was uncovered running next to the thirteenth-century Cross Wall. The line of stones on which the façade of the rampart was built can still be seen.

The smaller of the two rooms has a sloping paved floor leading to a drain, which suggests it may have been a 'stable' (établyi in Jèrriais) – probably for milch cows. There was a narrow stairway leading up to the wall walk at the end of the stable.

The arched doorway led from this undercroft directly to the stairwell leading to the Chambers above the Long Cellar (these can also be reached by walking around the base of the keep). Tucked behind the Cross Wall, they and the associated side chamber pose as many questions as does the vaulted Long Cellar below.

Gregg Wagstaff's sound installation based on the Latin Mass revisits the idea that this area was once seen as a medieval chapel.

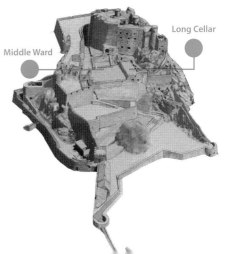

Long Cellar

Middle Ward

The Middle Ward

The side chamber built against the Cross Wall and the gateway has probably been open to the skies since the Civil War in the middle of the seventeenth century, while the existing walls seem to indicate that it was a guard chamber or wide corridor associated with the sally port. There was evidence of a sixteenth-century clay floor, but beneath this was a narrower corridor, which could be dated to the late thirteenth century.

The chamber over the Long Cellar was originally built as a single large room before it was later divided into three, each with its own fireplace in a recess in the wall. As in the Long Cellar below, a medieval altar was placed in the northern recess in 1915 to suggest its association with the Chapel of St George. A finely pointed, arched embrasure window looks out into the Lower Ward, and probably belongs to the first phase of this building.

A doorway in the west wall connected the chamber with the barracks, via the roof of the now lost corridor below.

A feature of the castle for over three centuries, this exterior staircase was demolished in 1911 and three years later the Georgian sashes were replaced by sixteenth-century-style stone-mullioned windows, as it was thought they improved the appearance of the Keep.

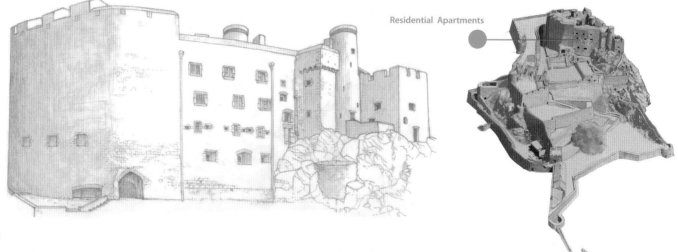

Residential Apartments

The Middle Ward

Base of the New Mount, tradesmen – Chris Bailey

From the Chamber over the Long Cellar it is possible to appreciate the massive bulk of the several buildings that make up the Keep – the best-protected part of the castle.

The base of the tower presents a number of mysteries. The Tudor builders appear to have constructed this massive structure on the remains of an earlier building, while the arched recess may have allowed a small cannon to command the stairs approaching the entrance to the Keep, and if this were the case then there must have been some sort of wall and doorway associated with it. The four-storey Residential Apartments were built in the mid-sixteenth century, and an external stair was subsequently built across the face of the building, giving access to the upper levels from the Middle Ward. When it was demolished in 1911, a doorway at the first level was blocked up and turned into a window.

The Corbelled Tower was probably built in the fifteenth century as additional accommodation. It had an oriel window, which was blocked when the Residential Apartments were built in the sixteenth century. During the French Wars (1793-1815) Philippe d'Auvergne converted the upper chamber into one of his reception rooms and built a glazed cupola on the roof.

Chris Bailey's sculpture represents the civilian presence within the castle. Throughout its history, a variety of tradesmen have visited the castle and the sculpture is a representation of John Wollehouse and Thomas Haddon, dyers from Coventry, whose visit to the castle was recorded in 1457.

At the eastern end of the Middle Ward Cross Wall is a windowless tower, overlooking the Cornish Bastion, which is known as the Prison Tower. The original was the easternmost tower of the thirteenth-century curtain wall, which was extended in the mid-Tudor period to carry a battery of guns commanding Grouville Bay. It would seem likely that the staircase leading down to the Bastion was separated by some kind of partition.

The building of the Tudor Residential Apartments obscured the domestic buildings of the medieval Keep. Only the South-East Tower and the corner of the Corbelled Tower remain free of the sixteenth-century attachments.

The Middle Ward

Prison Tower, prisoners – Bill Ming

The two-storey lodging tower known as the South-East Tower was built as part of the original Keep in the early thirteenth century and is also called Prynne's Tower after the Puritan politician/writer who was held prisoner in the castle between 1637 and 1640. The semi-circular wall at the base has the appearance of a small, ruined tower, which must have been accessed from above because there is no obvious way in. When it was excavated in the last century it was found to be filled with late seventeenth-century kitchen waste, which had been thrown from the doorway above.

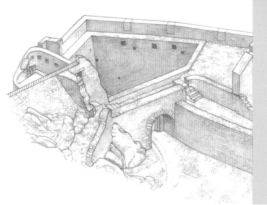

The three figures in Bill Ming's piece represent those unfortunates who spent time in the castle as prisoners. Again, this is a little known role of the castle – as an Island prison or even as a destination for England's most politically difficult prisoners. It was also the prison used to incarcerate those unfortunates who were identified as witches.

The Middle Ward

The Cornish Bastion, finished in 1547, housed cannon that controlled the Lower Ward and the northern end of Grouville Bay. A staircase inside the Curtain Wall from the Southern Flanking Tower and the Prison Tower accessed it and, as both are very narrow, it was easily defended. The powder and shot for the bastion's cannon were kept in a small powder house or magazine by the staircase.

Looking up from the Cornish Bastion towards the Prison Tower

Cornish Bastion, Tudor gunner – Chris Bailey

The introduction of cannon and gunpowder into warfare was a crucial phase in the development of Mont Orgueil, which really emerged as a gunpowder castle in the early sixteenth century. This is reflected by the replica of the Tudor artillery piece mounted in the embrasure of the Cornish Bastion, along with Chris Bailey's figure of a gunner

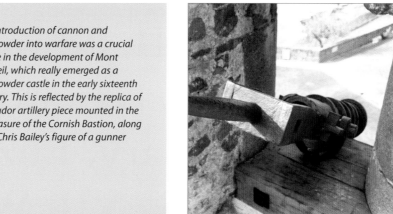

John, Henry III, Edward I. Edward II,
V, Henry VI, Edward IV, *Edward* V
Edward VI, Mary, Elizabeth I, James
II, James II & VII, William III & Ma
III, George IV, William IV, Victoria,

John, Henry III, Edward I. Edward II,
V, Henry VI, Edward IV, *Edward* V
Edward VI, Mary, Elizabeth I, James
II, James II & VII, William III & Ma
III, George IV, William IV, Victoria,

dward III, Richard II, Henry IV, Henry
Richard III, Henry VII, Henry VIII,
& VI, Charles I, *Inter-regnum*, Charles
II, Anne, George I, George II, George
dward VII, George V, Edward VIII,

dward III, Richard II, Henry IV, Henry
Richard III, Henry VII, Henry VIII,
& VI, Charles I, *Inter-regnum*, Charles
II, Anne, George I, George II, George
dward VII, George V, Edward VIII,

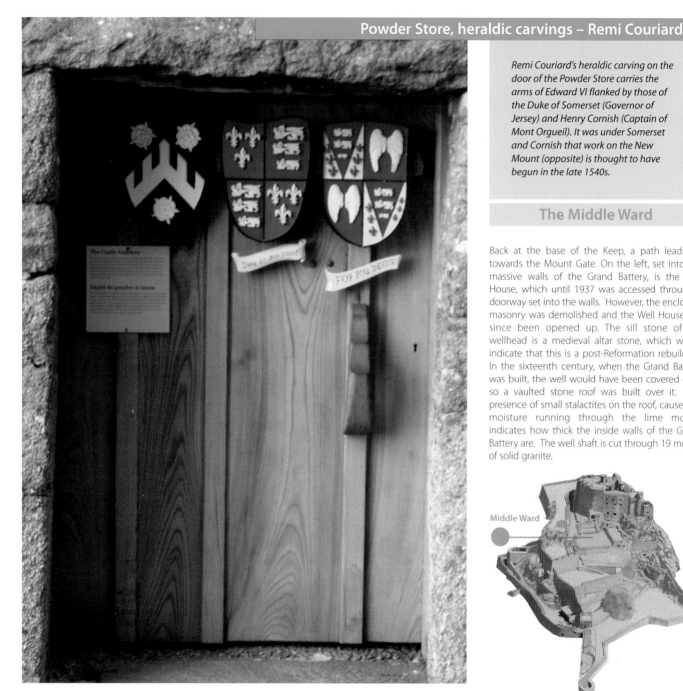

Remi Couriard's heraldic carving on the door of the Powder Store carries the arms of Edward VI flanked by those of the Duke of Somerset (Governor of Jersey) and Henry Cornish (Captain of Mont Orgueil). It was under Somerset and Cornish that work on the New Mount (opposite) is thought to have begun in the late 1540s.

The Middle Ward

Back at the base of the Keep, a path leads up towards the Mount Gate. On the left, set into the massive walls of the Grand Battery, is the Well House, which until 1937 was accessed through a doorway set into the walls. However, the enclosing masonry was demolished and the Well House has since been opened up. The sill stone of the wellhead is a medieval altar stone, which would indicate that this is a post-Reformation rebuilding. In the sixteenth century, when the Grand Battery was built, the well would have been covered over, so a vaulted stone roof was built over it. The presence of small stalactites on the roof, caused by moisture running through the lime mortar, indicates how thick the inside walls of the Grand Battery are. The well shaft is cut through 19 metres of solid granite.

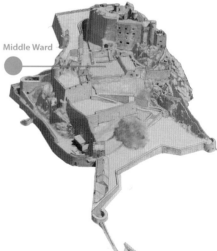

Middle Ward

At the head of the stairs the steps to the left lead to the Grand Battery, while the gateway on the right leads into the Keep.

Much of the organisation of the original north-east corner of the medieval castle has been lost under the massive bulk of the sixteenth-century Grand Battery. A large fourteenth-century fortification, still known in the 1590s as the Rochefort (after Sir John de Roches, its presumed builder), may have included the North-East Tower and remnants of other medieval defences now buried beneath the later Tudor works. These sixteenth-century additions on the north-east corner of the castle can be divided into the Inner Works and the Outer Works, and were accessed through the doorway and the covered stairway set into the wall at the head of the main stairs.

The Inner Works took the form of an arrowhead flanker, the guns of which protected the castle from any enemy approaching from the north. The Germans, who roofed the space during the Occupation, converted this into a barrack-room and observation post.

The Outer Works were reached through a small sally port and a series of steps. Today the main feature of these works is Caesar's Fort, which was probably built in the sixteenth century, although most of what remains is an eighteenth-century musketry platform.

Caesar's Fort, looking down from the Rampier

Well, 'good luck' coins – Gordon Young

The tradition of throwing money into water in return for good luck has its origins in the votive offerings made to appease the gods as early as the Bronze and Iron Ages. Gordon Young's exhibit reflects how this tradition has carried on even to the present day, as all the coins in the glass jar were collected from the bottom of the well.

The Middle Ward

The nature of warfare changed with the introduction of field artillery, and the design of castles had to reflect this. Enemies could threaten the castle by placing their cannon on Mont St Nicolas opposite, so during the second half of the sixteenth century the Grand Battery, or Rampier, was built by the Paulet governors to counter this. It replaced the medieval curtain wall and interval towers, and served as a platform for guns.

Grand Battery, artillery – Royal Armouries and local craftsmen

The replica Tudor artillery pieces on the Grand Battery, made by Island craftsmen, and the Mount Battery, made by the Royal Armouries, highlight this crucial phase in the development of Mont Orgueil. The earliest reference to gunpowder in the castle dates from 1326, when sulphur vivium (Living Sulphur) was mentioned, although this was probably fired as flaming darts by ballista rather than cannon. (The earliest reference to an iron gun was in 1372 and cannon and coulverines were first mentioned in 1462.)

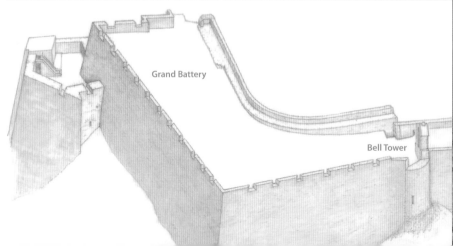

Grand Battery

Bell Tower

Bell Tower, 'King Death' – Stephen Gumbley

The Bell Tower was one of the original thirteenth-century interval towers and had a doorway at its base that led into the Middle Ward. When the battery was built, the tower was heightened and two gun ports were added. Powder and shot would have been stored in a small magazine built behind it in the thickness of the walls. When the southernmost end of the Rampier was built onto the thirteenth-century Western Flanking Tower, a gunner's room and magazine was built behind it to service the guns on the Paul Ivy Bulwark. From this vantage point, the vaulted roof of the Iron Gate with its associated wall walk built in front of the St George's Gate in the late thirteenth or early fourteenth century can clearly be seen.

Returning to the Keep, one can appreciate the size and bulk of the sixteenth-century additions to the fourth and final part of the castle – the Keep itself.

Stephen Gumbley's exhibit in the Bell Tower uses models and a light installation to focus on the theme of death in the medieval world. The Black Death of 1349 and subsequent plagues, coupled with the ever-present threat of French attack, meant that, to medieval Islanders, death was always close at hand. The exhibit uses figures drawn from the medieval wall painting in St Clement's Church of Les Trois Vifs et Trois Morts ('The Three Living and the Three Dead').

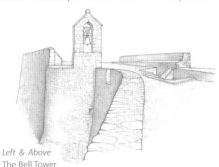

Left & Above
The Bell Tower

Grand Battery, the Garrison – Chris Bailey and Gordon Young

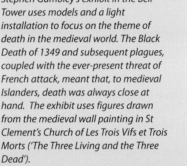

Chris Bailey's figures manning the ramparts represent the unnamed soldiers of the castle's garrison over the centuries. They represent an English crossbowman of 1224, the first year in which crossbows are mentioned in relation to Mont Orgueil, a Jersey archer of 1340 and a Norman arquebusier of 1468. (The arquebus was an early form of hand-gun.) Associated with the figures, Gordon Young's stones carry the names of over 400 men in the garrison in 1337–1345, the early years of the Hundred Years War.

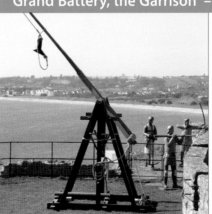

The doorway into the North-East Tower from the Grand Battery was inserted in the late sixteenth century. A third entrance to the Keep was created when a doorway (now blocked) was added into the second floor of the Residential Apartments. This was connected to the Middle Ward by a flight of stairs.

Today this means that there are essentially two routes visitors can take to reach the highest point of the castle – the Medieval and the Tudor.

The Keep from the Mount Battery

The Mount Gate entrance to the Keep

The Keep

Originally built on the highest part of the rocky promontory, the size of the buildings of the Keep was determined by the width of the ridge. Minor changes were carried out to the Keep in the fifteenth century, but it was extensively remodelled in the sixteenth century during the governorships of Edward Seymour and the Paulet family, when a new lodging range was added, along with a new Great Chamber, and the entire building was protected from cannon fire by the construction of the New Mount, which served as a barrier for increased security.

The present entrance to the Keep is through the Mount Gate, which was probably built in the fifteenth century as part of a two-storey guardhouse. The portcullis slots in the side of the gateway were blocked when an extra storey was added to it in 1551, along with the windows and inscription above the gateway. An arrow loop in the western wall of the Long Passage may indicate the presence of a forebuilding leading to the original medieval Keep.

The Medieval Route

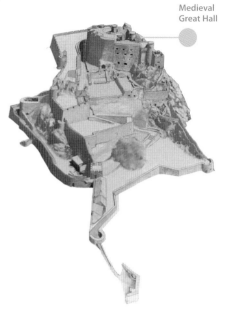

North-East Tower

The North-East Tower was originally built in the thirteenth century as a two-storey lodging tower situated at the north-east corner of the medieval Keep. It has its own garderobe (lavatory) with its own window for ventilation on the upper floor. It was adapted to take cannon in the late sixteenth or early seventeenth century, when the tower was filled with earth to the level of the floor and gunports pierced the walls. However, this fill was removed in the early eighteenth century and the tower was turned into a magazine to store gunpowder

A passage linked the tower with the Medieval Hall, and at some stage in the late fifteenth or early sixteenth century, gun ports were added to control the approaches to the Mount Gate. Although the passage is open-topped, there is evidence of an earlier timber roof.

The North-East passage

Medieval Great Hall

The Medieval Hall is the most significant survival of the castle's medieval accommodation, and over the centuries has had many different roles, which might have included both religious and domestic use.

Mystery Two – Medieval Hall or Chapel?

Although this guide describes the large vaulted chamber in the Medieval Keep as the Hall, there is an alternative school of thought which believes that it may have been the original castle chapel. The opposing view is based upon the perceived weakness of the walls and the unusual style of the hipped/vaulted roof combined with the relative small size of the room. The dimensions of the building which was popularly known in the eighteenth century as 'the Old Church' are similar to those of 'the platform of the chapel' (40 x 20ft), as recorded in 1573.

However, measured against this is the fact that the building's location on the summit of the ridge determines the width of the building but gives it the strongest position within the castle and the Courtauld Institute's study has shown that the wall paintings are of a secular nature.

Medieval Great Hall

Originally built in the thirteenth century, this building was at the heart of the medieval castle. Lit by two windows in each of the long walls, and by a fifth in the north gable, the room was probably floored in timber and may have had a steeply pitched roof. A later spiral staircase in the north-east corner of the room led up through the roof to the wall-walk and parapets that topped the building. The main entrance to the hall was in the middle of the west wall and two other doors led to the North-East and South-East towers. The existing vaulted roof probably dates to the fourteenth century, and the fireplace in the south wall may originally have been built at this time. In 2004, wall paintings, which have since been dated to about 1500 by the Courtauld Institute, were uncovered in several places. In the Tudor period new buildings were added to the west and one of the windows was converted into a doorway to access the new Residential Apartments. At some stage a central hearth and drain were inserted into the room, which may suggest the space was used as a kitchen for some time. A beehive-shaped oven in the east wall also dates from this period. In 1778–9 the room was converted into a barrack room for 60 men by General Conway, at which time the two windows in the east wall were enlarged, the vault was repaired, and the fireplace was rebuilt. In 2004 the hall was restored to how it may have looked in the late medieval period.

The wall painting being exposed

Below
The Medieval Hall

Medieval Hall, Wheel of Fortune – Brian Fell

Brian Fell's Wheel of Fortune exhibit represents a common medieval image of the price of power, and is inspired by the illustrated medieval manuscript Roman de la Rose that was stolen from the Jersey Library in 1955.

Medieval Hall, Tree of Succession – Brian Fell

Brian Fell's intricate Tree of Succession exhibit shows the complexity of the dynastic relationships between the French and English royal families, starting with Eleanor of Aquitaine and the Plantagenet kings of England, that led to the Hundred Years War (1337–1453). The inspiration for the style of exhibits comes from the medieval tree of Jesse tradition, which in turn influenced the family tree used by genealogists.

Medieval Great Hall

The Undercroft

The spiral staircase in the north-east corner of the room leads down to the Undercroft. The width of the natural rock determined how big the medieval builders could make the Keep, as the ridge falls steeply away on both sides. A relieving arch in the south wall shows that good building space was limited here at the top of the castle. When it was originally built, in the first half of the thirteenth century, the Undercroft had wooden beams that stretched from wall to wall; the vaulted roof with its three pillars had been added by the fourteenth century. From the sixteenth century, a number of changes took place: the pillars were thickened and a doorway and steps were added to give access to the lowest floor of the Residential Apartments. An altar was reinstated in 2004 to reflect the space's possible religious use.

The large external windows are not original medieval features and can only have been added at a much later date, possibly in the eighteenth century. It was during that century that a section of vaulting collapsed and a supporting wall was added.

Above
The Undercroft, showing the bulky column and altar

The Corbelled Tower

Returning to the Medieval Hall by the spiral stairs, cross over to the doorway in the south-east corner which leads through to the Corbelled Tower. This was built on the highest point of the castle rock. In its existing form, it probably dates from the late fifteenth century and was a two-storey accommodation block between the Medieval Hall and the South-East Tower. There may have been an earlier structure on this site.

The fireplace was restored in the 1920s, when the tower was gutted, the floors and roofs were renewed and internal doorways were altered. The oriel window on this floor, glazed only in the centre, was lost in the sixteenth century, when the Residential Apartments and the connecting spiral Stair Tower were built.

It is thought that the tower was used as the castle hospital in the late eighteenth century. In the 1630s the political prisoner, William Prynne, had his lodgings here and in the adjoining South-East Tower.

Corbelled Tower 2, Sir Walter Raleigh – Ronnie Heeps

Ronnie Heeps's installation combines paintings and an 'electronic book' to represent the story of Sir Walter Raleigh, described by historian G R Balleine as Jersey's most distinguished governor. Raleigh's importance to the castle was in intervening to prevent its demolition when the new castle in St Aubin's Bay was built. However, Raleigh's real importance is that he links Jersey with the wider world of the Renaissance at a time when the Island was on the threshold of its New World adventure that would bring it such wealth in the ensuing centuries.

The Corbelled Tower

Medieval physicians often made a diagnosis based upon the colour of their patient's urine, and to help them they carried a small circular card on which the varying colours were shown. Gordon Young's exhibit mounted in the garderobe of the South-East Tower has created this card in reality

The South-East Tower

The doorway leads directly into the second floor of the South-East Tower, which was built as a two-storey structure with a battlemented roof as part of the original Keep. Like other towers in the castle, it provided lodgings for the garrison; the grandest room, on the top floor, had its own garderobe. The lower chamber is reached by a short outside staircase. In the late fifteenth century it was decorated with wall paintings and may have been used as a small private oratory. Conservation of the few remaining fragments of painted wall plaster was carried out in 1999. After the mid-sixteenth century the tower was converted to take artillery and the lower chamber was completely filled in with clay to create a solid platform – new gun ports were formed in the walls at the level where the original timber floor had been.

The South-East Tower

The roof of the tower can be reached by taking the spiral stairs. Looking through the battlements, visitors have a commanding view of the lower parts of the castle and Grouville Bay. The spiral stairs continue on to the roof and then to the Mount Battery, while a door leads into the top floor of the Corbelled Tower with its west-facing oriel window overlooking the Middle Ward. When it was built in the fifteenth century there were glazed lights on all three sides of the projecting bay, not just in the centre, and the splayed sides had stone benches.

A view from the roof of the South-East Tower

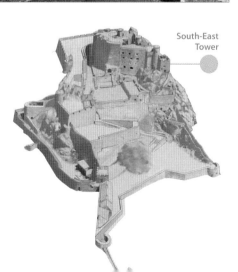

Prayer nuts were devotional objects carried by wealthy Christians in the late medieval period. Some were made of silver or gold, but most were carved from wood. They were often carried on the end of the rosary. The exteriors of prayer nuts were elaborately carved and pierced, with a cavity to hold perfume. The halves of the prayer nut opened to reveal roundels with carved religious scenes, which the owners would study to inspire their worship.

For this commission, the artist Steve Manthorp was asked to create twelve prayer nuts of scenes to show the importance of the Virgin Mary, the mother of Christ, and Saint George to the history of Mont Orgueil and Jersey.

In the middle of the sixteenth century this chamber lost its position as the principal chamber in the castle when the new Residential Apartments were built alongside. The new inner spiral staircase (built to serve the new range) obstructed the bay window, and so a smaller opening was inserted to the left of the bay. During the first years of the nineteenth century Philippe d'Auvergne used the chamber as one of his reception rooms, built a glazed cupola on the roof and had a niche for a statue let into the northern wall.

The doorway in the west wall leads onto the spiral staircase and the Tudor Apartments.

South-East Tower

The Tudor Route

The Mount Gate – entrance to the Keep

As the first stages of this work were being carried out, the hunting frieze which decorated the arch of the gateway was damaged and an inscription, dated 1551, was inserted just above it. The portcullis was removed and windows were cut into the Portcullis Chamber walls to allow light to pass into the Long Passage behind. On the east side of the Long Passage is the thirteenth-century hall, while the west wall incorporates an arrow loop and other features of an early barbican or forebuilding of some kind.

The Tudor Keep is entered through the final gate within the castle – the Mount Gate. It was built in the fifteenth century as a two-storey gatehouse (entered by the door on the right) and the entrance was secured with gates and a portcullis operated from a Portcullis Chamber above. The lower floor was a guardroom with lodging above. The fireplace in the south wall originally had a lintel made from a recycled altar stone, but this was removed and given to the cathedral at Trenton, New Jersey, in 1950. When the New Mount was built in the sixteenth century the nature of the gatehouse changed, and the rear wall was demolished and the Long Passage was created. An extra storey was added to the guardhouse, but it was only accessible from the new Great Chamber.

HOSTES NICOLLE PORTER 1551

The Tudor Route

During the sixteenth century the Long Passage had two sets of stairs, but a sloping floor and 11 steps replaced them in the eighteenth century. The niches on either side of the passage were added in about 1800, when Philippe d'Auvergne, Prince de Bouillon, used the castle as the base for his spy network. This roof of the passage was finally replaced in 2005, having been open to the elements for many years.

The second doorway on the right-hand side of the passage leads directly into the Undercroft of the Great Chamber. This would have been used for storage, and three unglazed windows allowed light to filter through from the Long Passage. A narrow doorway leads into a space that originally contained four floors and had a flat lead roof. The positions of the floors and roof are clearly identified by scars in the walls. The first and second floors were entered directly from the Great Chamber, but it is still uncertain how these rooms were used, although they were possibly service areas. The third floor was reached across the roof through a narrow exterior doorway and was probably a magazine (gunpowder store) for the cannon placed on the Mount Battery

Apartments 1, witches in the castle – Mike Woods

Mike Woods's exhibits highlight the castle's position during the witch hysteria that overtook Protestant Europe in the sixteenth and seventeenth centuries. Historian G R Balleine lists 65 witch trials in the Island between 1562 and 1660, and many of the accused were incarcerated in the castle. As sorcery was taken to be a pact with the Devil, Mike Woods has created a Devil set behind a screen, on which figures are made to move by visitors turning handles.

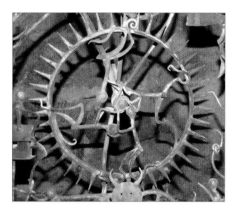

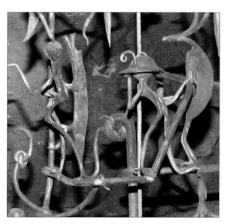

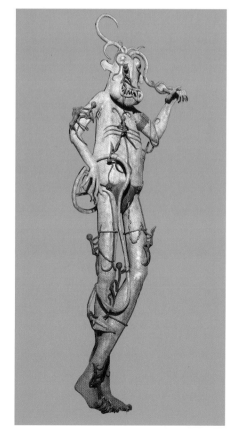

The Tudor Route

The doorway on the left-hand side leads into the Undercroft of the Medieval Hall, and from there down a steep staircase into the ground floor of the Tudor Residential Apartments. The three small, undecorated windows were clearly designed as gun ports rather than windows, but when the stone staircase was built across the face of the Residential Apartments, two of the gun ports were blocked and the third was made into a doorway. These were only reopened following the demolition of the stairs in 1911.

Apartments 3, arms video – Brian Fell & Josh Young

In the former Governor's chamber on the fourth floor of the Residential Apartments, Brian Fell has created a stunning support for the screen onto which Josh Young's video project is shown. The subject of the video is the arms and armour that would have been used in the castle, while the screen is made up of a series of replica pieces of armour and weaponry.

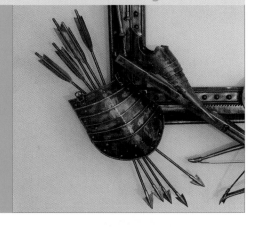

The range was stripped of its nineteenth-century additions during the second two decades of the twentieth century. This third floor is divided by a timber-framed partition, with the antechamber being no more than a corridor leading to the inner spiral staircase and the Long Passage, and linking through a new door into the Medieval Hall. A large fireplace set into the northern wall heated the chamber on this floor. From the antechamber, the spiral staircase leads down to the second floor of the Residential Apartments, which was probably designed as officers' quarters and was a plain room with a simple fireplace and entrance in the east wall. The room is lit by three single-light windows made from Caen stone, each flanked by a pair of gun ports. The doorway on the staircase leads to the now demolished outside staircase which led down into the Middle Ward.

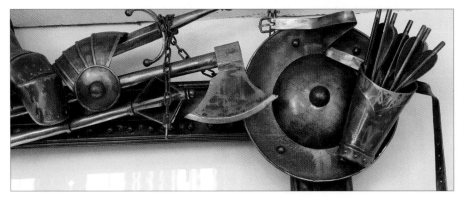

This staircase also leads up to the fourth floor of the Residential Apartments, which contains the largest and finest chamber in the castle and which may have been known as 'the Captain's Chamber'. Divided by a timber-framed partition, the smaller antechamber has one window and a small plain fireplace with the name 'R. Warwick', captain of the castle in the 1650s, scratched into the lintel. The principal chamber has two windows and a typical Tudor fireplace with decorated spandrels.

When it was built, the windows had walk-in embrasures with narrow stone seats along either side, but in the late eighteenth-century cannon were mounted in them. Soon after, in the early nineteenth century, Philippe d'Auvergne demolished the partition and converted the chamber and antechamber into a grand reception room. He lowered the sills of the Tudor windows and inserted late Georgian sash windows. These were removed in 1914, when the windowsills and mullions were restored to what was then believed to be their Tudor form.

The Tudor Route

Fourth floor of the Residential Apartments
Portrait of Sir Anthony Paulet

The Great Chamber

Leading from this room, a doorway goes directly into the Great Chamber. This large chamber, created when the New Mount was built, was called 'St George's Hall' on the Manson plan of 1755, and has come to be known more recently as the Tudor Great Hall. The floor was probably tiled originally, and its comparatively modest off-centre fireplace could once have had a carved oak chimney piece. The main source of natural light came from a range of windows in the east wall, where the jambs of the two end windows can still be seen. The internal walls would have been plastered, and there is some evidence of a possible painted frieze at a high level on the south wall.

There are five windows in the west wall. The four that are arranged symmetrically around the fireplace may have been plastered, because three of them are made from Caen stone, while the fourth is granite. This may have been because of the need for a roof beam. A fifth window carried a small quatrefoil (possibly a recycled medieval ecclesiastical feature), which let light into the stairway behind.

The Chamber had fallen into ruin by the end of the eighteenth century, and part of it was being used as a kitchen by Philippe d'Auvergne. Its ruination was completed in the 1920s, when the last of the roof beams were removed. The present roof and floor and the eastern window range were rebuilt in 2005.

Equanimity by Chris Levine

This 3D portrait of Her Majesty, by artist Chris Levine, was commissioned to hang in the Great Chamber at Mont Orgueil (at that stage still in the planning process) as part of the Jersey 1204-2004 celebrations, which marked the 800th anniversary of Jersey's special relationship with the English Crown. In order to create this iconic portrait, Chris Levine enlisted some of the world's finest holographers, Dr John Perry, Robert Munday and Jeffery Robb. Together they have pushed the boundaries of this imaging technique. Using a camera specially commissioned for the task and designed by Munday and Robb, they took over 10,000 images and 3D data-sets of Her Majesty during two sittings

The portrait is intended to represent the idea of La Reine, Notre Duc, which is a popular loyal toast in Jersey that refers both to the English royal connection and the Island's ancient allegiance to the Duke of Normandy. Mont Orgueil was a royal castle, an interest that Her Majesty only renounced in 1996. Formal royal images can appear distant and aloof, but Equanimity reflects the contemporary relevance of the Island's constitutional traditions by using 21st century technology to create a very strong sense of the living person.

The Tudor Route

In addition to the doorway leading into the Great Chamber from the Residential Apartments, a pair of doors in the west wall give access to store rooms beyond, while a door in the north wall leads into the Guard Tower. This chamber was built on top of the fifteenth-century Guard Tower as part of the sixteenth-century reorganisation and reconstruction of the Keep. The recess in the wall was probably a 'keeping place' – an early form of cupboard. The focal point of the room is the fireplace set in the south wall. The window, with its decorated moulding and integral seat, is made of Caen stone and also served as a gun port in the event of a siege. The doorway in the north-east corner of the room leads to the chamber over the gateway.

Guardroom 3, Puritanism: Golden Chair – Gordon Young

Gordon Young's Golden Chair exhibit is an interpretation of the Tudor morality tale, The Most Wonderful and Strange Finding of a Chayre of Gold, Neare the Isle of Iarse, in which the key event was set just off the coast from Mont Orgueil.

In the darkest recesses of the castle, at the heart of the Keep, David Kemp's 'Fabulous Beasts' highlight the role of the mythical creatures in the medieval world. The shrine to the Melusine points to the mythical origins of the Plantagenet kings, while the dragon was often used in popular culture to portray a protector of treasure or as a symbol of destructive forces. The griffin combined the strength and nobility of the lion, the king of the beasts, with the ability to fly and the excellent eyesight of the eagle, the king of the skies, to create the ideal composite creature.

Returning to the Great Chamber, access to the roof of the Residential Apartments is by the spiral staircase. This emerges onto the timber gun deck, which overlooks what is arguably the best landing beach in the Island for an invader. Artillery placed here has commanded the anchorage since the sixteenth century. This new timber deck lies on great oak beams fixed into the original Tudor parapet just above the lead roof. The lead roofs lying beneath were replaced in 2002, and during this work a great deal of evidence for the position of the beams, parapet gutters and lead flashings was revealed.

Gundeck on the Residential Apartments, seaward viewing table – Russell Coleman

The views from the top of the castle have always been an important part of the visitor's experience of Mont Orgueil, and Russell Coleman's three relief models carved in stone show the significance of the location of the castle at different levels. The first shows the strategic importance of the Channel Islands with regard to Medieval France, the second shows the relationship of the castle with the Island, and the final model shows the castle's tactical position.

The Mount Battery

The octagonal turret here has changed size and shape quite dramatically over the years. In the eighteenth century it was part of a chain of signal stations used to relay messages between patrolling warships and Guernsey. During the Occupation, when it was raised by about a metre and used as an observation post, the concrete top would have been painted to look like the surrounding granite.

Several of the paving stones on the battery have consecration crosses cut into them, suggesting that they were once medieval altar slabs – another indication that the battery was built after the Reformation. The cannon placed here were supplied with powder and shot from a magazine in the top floor of the rooms built behind the bulk of the New Mount, which was reached via the roof of the Great Chamber.

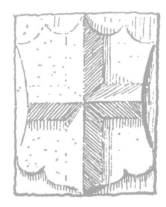

The stair towers were heightened during the Occupation to take observation posts.

The shields around the top of the Mount Battery that feature the cross of St George are believed to have been carved from Caen stone taken from religious houses demolished during the Reformation.

The highest point of the castle, the Mount Battery, is reached by a short staircase. As well as sheltering the Residential Apartments and other accommodation within the Keep, the Mount Battery provided a substantial and stable base for cannon to counter any threat from Mont St Nicolas opposite.

The Exhibits

Although the exhibition appears to be made up of a series of stand-alone exhibits scattered throughout the castle, there is in fact a central theme running through them all and that is the Medieval World and Jersey's place in it. The exhibits look at the various contexts in which the castle can be seen and these are loosely arranged according to the medieval idea of 'The Great Chain of Being'. This idea meant that everything had its rightful place in Creation, with the rocks of the earth at the bottom, gradually rising in importance through plants and animals to humans, until one reached the Heavens and the Glory of God.

1. Chris Bailey
2. Russel Coleman
3. Remi Couriard
4. Owen Cunningham
5. Brian Fell
6. Andy Frost
7. Steve Gumbley
8. Ronnie Heeps
9. David Kemp
10. Chris Levine
11. Neil Mahrer
12. Steve Manthorp
13. Mark Griffin
14. Bill Ming and Stan Bullard
15. Mike Woods
16. Gregg Wagstaff
17. Dixie-Lee Whiteman
18. Gordon Young
19. Josh Young

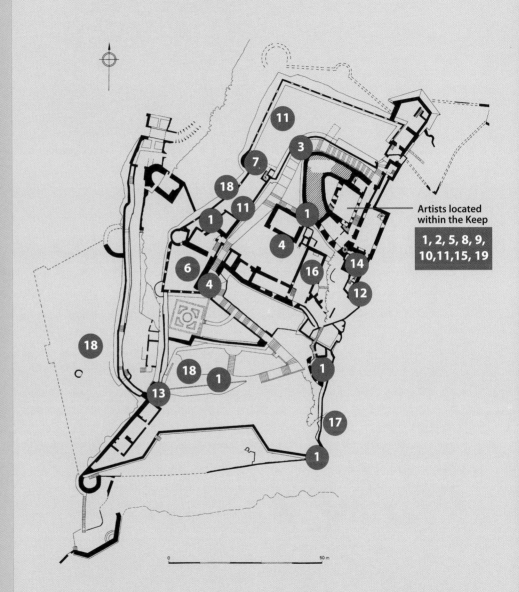

Artists located within the Keep

1, 2, 5, 8, 9, 10, 11, 15, 19

Chris Bailey:
Wood carvings of human figures and outdoor furniture

The body of work that I was commissioned to make can be split into two distinct groups: human figures and outdoor furniture detailing certain elements of the natural history of the Island. All the pieces have been constructed from oak and hand-carved. The furniture is inspired by traditional designs found in illustrations from the medieval period, although the sea bench takes inspiration from the ribs of a boat and rock pools.

One of the first things that I did was to immerse myself in the European medieval period by travelling to see with my own eyes the art and architecture in countries such as Spain and Switzerland, as well as the UK. Further study was mostly book-based. This research allowed me to develop an understanding of the evolution of clothing and also of the weaponry and armour that would have been common during the period covered.

In making the figures, I have tried to capture the essence of the medieval sculpture that I have so enjoyed studying.

Russel Coleman:
Viewing tables

Like the castle itself, the materials and techniques used to produce the artworks were a combination of the latest technology available, mixed with some of the oldest skills known. As an artist in the twenty-first century, I have been able to martial the use of tooling that includes diamonds, tungsten, ultra-high-pressure abrasive water jet, and heat-resistant ceramics to shape wood, stone and metal. Although modern machines have primarily shaped the wood and stone, they were still hand-carved and finished in much the same way as has been done for numerous centuries, and bronze casting still remains the same process that it was thousands of years ago.

Ever since humans first created images, we have used them to place ourselves in time and space, and making sense of what we do and why we do it. The only difference here is the use of the ultra-modern techniques to celebrate a time and place 800 years ago and events pre-dating the castle. They are used here to show why the castle is where it is, firstly illustrating the geopolitics of time and the strategic importance of Jersey's physical position in relation to both England and France; secondly, the castle's position in relation to the Island; and finally, the defensive position of the castle with relation to the ballistic capabilities of the time and the growth of the castle in relation to ongoing capabilities.

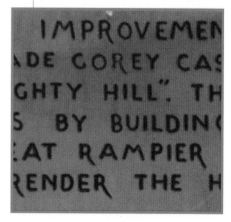

Remi Couriard:
(Official Heraldic Carver to the New Zealand Government)
Carved door and benches

The carved door

This commission was undertaken in close conjunction with JHT staff, and then with Timothy Duke, Chester Herald (College of Arms, London).
The door is made up of elm, as records show that 70 tons of elm was used in the construction of Mont Orgueil during the period that Edward Seymour and Henry Cornish were in office.
The three heraldic carvings of arms are those 'missing' from Somerset Tower:
Edward VI
Edward Seymour
Henry Cornish

The ten solid-oak benches with a natural tung oil finish

The shape of the seat is taken from the view captured from the heights of the Keep. The curved seating planks reflect the sight of the waves advancing along the Royal Bay of Grouville towards the shore.
The heavy under-frame and legs represent the heavy timbers used at the Gates and Drawbridges.
The open construction shows the honesty of workmanship and joinery and also allows the timber to move with the extremes of weather conditions.
Timber used – English oak

Owen Cunningham:
The 'Sir Hugh' Project

Although the research for the Sir Hugh Project was fascinating, it was also very daunting. Could my skills as a metalworker match those fourteenth-century armourers who were at the cutting edge of technology? Once I realised that my role was that of sculptor and not as a would-be armourer, then I relaxed and began to really enjoy the challenge. I decided at once that the horse would have to be 'alive' and be fully part of the piece, not a plastic support for a suit of armour. Also, Sir Hugh himself was a man inside protective layers and so we should 'feel' his life within. Horses and riders are fully aware of each other and I wanted to capture that connectedness in a sculptural way.

The Wound Man

The Wound Man involved a return to wood sculpture for me. To cope with such a large-scale project, I enlisted the assistance of chainsaw artist Andrew Frost, who blocked out the figure from the assembled oak trunks, following a life-size polystyrene model that I had made.

The figure on its base stands at over 5 metres high and is braced by a galvanised steel armature. The armature includes a jib hoist, which lifts the heavy oak elements into position in the confines of Elizabeth Gate. In an essentially two-dimensional image, I have striven to preserve the naivete of draughtsmanship often found in the barber-surgeon's notebooks.

Brian Fell:
Metalwork sculptures

In trying to show the complicated family relationship between the kings of France and England, the medieval imagery invoked by the tree of Jesse suggested the form of the metalwork Tree of Succession. The difficulty of creating the heads when no accurate likeness exists of the people concerned, apart from coins and medieval illustrations, was overcome by dressing the heads in headgear appropriate to the age.

The Wheel of Fortune was widely used as an allegory in medieval literature and art to aid religious instruction. The wheel served to remind people of the temporality of earthly things and showed that even kings and emperors cannot escape bad luck - today's king could be tomorrow's beggar. There was an illustration of the Wheel of Fortune in an ancient Jersey manuscript called the Romance of the Rose, which was dated to around 1230 but which sadly was stolen from St Helier's public library in 1955. The only reference to it that we have is a black and white photograph taken in the 1920s.

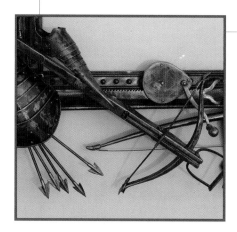

Andy Frost:
Playground sculptor

The building of the castle required a variety of craftsmen and labourers, only few of whom are remembered and named in documents from the time. The names and roles of some of these have been carved into the simple figures used to carry the play equipment. Medieval illustrations show the type of equipment used in the building of the castle – ramps, ladders, wheels, pulleys and scaffolding – and these all lend themselves to the creation of a children's play area and allows information about the medieval builders to be passed on in a subliminal way.

Steve Gumbley:
Shadow sculpture

People of the fourteenth and fifteenth centuries witnessed death more than we do today. It was an ever-present threat, a shadow over life from birth to old age. This was reflected in the popular stories of that time, with vivid images of dancing skeletons and decaying corpses providing strong reminders of mortality.

The starting points of this exhibit are these grisly warnings and the fact that the Bell Tower Chamber was used by archers or crossbowmen, who defended the castle through window slits.

Viewed from above, it shows the castle dominated by the 'King of Death' and surrounded by deathly figures, all casting shadows over the castle and onto the walls of the chamber. Revolving slowly, like a prayer wheel, this is a mechanical meditation on darkness and light, death and life.

Constructed in steel, wood and fibreglass, with help from Andy Plant and Bryan Tweddle. Music by David Humpage.

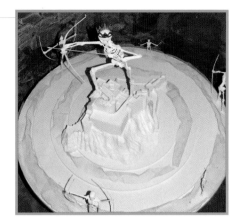

Ronnie Heeps:
Sir Walter Raleigh

I chose Sir Walter Raleigh, as he was a former Governor of the Island and was a typical Renaissance man. He shared a 'world view', which would eventually end the medieval period. In 1600, Queen Elizabeth I sent Sir Walter to Jersey with instructions to demolish Mont Orgueil Castle. He was supposed to use its stone to build a bigger, more defensible castle. When Raleigh arrived he realised that Mont Orgueil was worth saving and he sent a letter to the Queen stating: 'It is a stately fort of great capacity and I consider it a pity to cast it down.' Raleigh was the consummate Renaissance man; he excelled in numerous fields and was able to cross between the disciplines of arts and sciences with ease. He was not afraid to undertake daring deeds and dream of a glorious multifaceted world, which lay just beyond the horizon of conventional thought. It is a reasonable assumption to state that the Renaissance man was the first to comprehend a future world that was not a preordained construct, and one that was in a constant state of flux and open to the influence of secular thinkers.

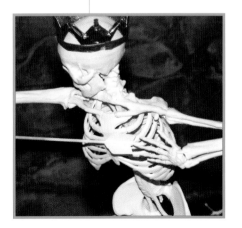

David Kemp (from Museum of Mythology):
Three medieval mythological creatures

I work in an 'assemblage' process. I collect and recycle all sorts of discarded items. When things have been thrown away their functions are similarly discarded, and I combine them in new contexts, discovering new identities for them.

These three exhibits illustrate medieval mythological creatures connected with Mont Orgueil: the Griffin, part-lion, part-eagle; the Dragon; and the Melusine, half- woman, half-serpent.

The components of these displays hint at the character and function of the creature.

The Dragon has been reconstructed from fragments of carved wood, wrought iron, carthorse harnesses and musical instruments, evocative of some sort of medieval mechanical dragon that might have been used in theatrical processions.

The Griffin is made from bamboo and papier-mâché, lightweight materials suitable for depicting it as it swoops from aloft.

The fabulous Melusine is immortal. Her shrine-like collection of memorabilia contains, among other items, a pair of snakeskin high-heels, still in fashion amongst snake-women and a reminder that she may still be with us.

Changing beliefs – medieval myths

Throughout history, societies have collected relics from the past, and presented them to illustrate contemporary beliefs. History is constantly being rewritten, and 'explanations' are constantly being revised.

The medieval world was deeply superstitious, as very little had been 'proven' in scientific terms. Dragons, griffins, fairies and goblins were as 'real' to them as God or hell-fire. Medieval minds were open to belief; anything was possible.

In the nineteenth century, the age of Enlightenment examined medieval beliefs in the light of scientific enquiry, and many myths were dismissed as mere superstition. Rational explanations were constructed for the endurance of fragments from the past.

Myths, however, endure, occupying spaces in the human mind beyond the rational. Archetypes persist. Here 'there still be monsters', representing things that we do not quite believe but still do not yet know. Objects may be revealed to be 'fakes', but science has not yet provided all the 'real' answers.

The Melusine is most particular both to the locality of Jersey and North-West France, and to Mont Orgueil with its Plantagenet associations. It is also the most mysterious and, as it is immortal, perhaps the most contemporary.

The Melusine was a beautiful woman who, from the waist down, was a terrible serpent. When her suspicious husband spied her in the bath one Saturday, she shrieked, defenestrated and disappeared. Throughout the ages this creature still watches over her descendants, warning them when disasters threaten.

This little shrine contains fragments, relics and photos which might well have been collected by devotees of a secret Melusine cult. The snake woman is immortal, a pair of snakeskin high-heels seems very fashionable, a reminder that she might still be with us. Yesssssssss.

The Dragon is a persistent creature, occurring throughout many of the world's mythologies. It appears in medieval stories and throughout medieval heraldry. There are several legends of particular dragons indigenous to Jersey.

Whether they really existed or not, dragons were an integral part of the medieval world's imagination. Dragon-like creatures would have been constructed to simulate their supernatural powers. This wooden dragon might well be the reconstructed fragments of a theatrical monster. Whether he was designed to represent the awesome fire-breathing powers of dragons or merely to hoodwink the gullible is not certain.

The Griffin, half-lion, half-eagle, was an important medieval creature, with symbolism associated with the sun and Christianity. Sir John Mandeville, a medieval writer, describes one as such: '… for he hath large nayles on his fete, as great as it were horns of oxen, and of those they make cups there to drink of, and his ribs they make bowes to shoot with.'

Chris Levine:
Portrait of Her Majesty the Queen
(lenticule)

Equanimity was my working title for the commission and came to me in a purely intuitive manner. As I developed the work it became increasingly pertinent to me, and I asked Her Majesty whether the piece could be titled as such. She felt it was appropriate. I first came across the word in the context of my practice of meditation, where the primary objective is to be still and attain harmony of being through an equanimous state of mind. My experience of *vipassana* meditation was something I shared with Her Majesty in explaining my thinking behind the title. I was very conscious of the breathing rhythm of my subject when recording the images, as each sequence required Her Majesty to remain still for around eight seconds. I believe that in doing so I caught the subject in an almost meditative state of pause where the truth is allowed to manifest. I had asked her to fix her gaze during the exposures on an ultra-violet cross floating inside a transparent cube. She is after all the head of the Church of England.

In developing the work I wanted to distil it to pure essence. I resisted the use of props and iconography and chose to create an image which was in itself a modern icon. In the two sittings I had with the Queen I shot some several thousand digital images and also captured the bust of Her Majesty in 360 degrees as a computer model. I chose the final image with Her Majesty at Windsor and she took a keen interest in the project. *Equanimity* now represents a body of work that will manifest in time in ever-changing light forms, but with a continuity of sentiment. I think this well represents the objectives of the commission as a statement of the relationship between the monarch and the Island of Jersey that has endured over the last 800 years and is still strong in this new millennium.

In order to create this historic portrait, I worked with some of the finest holographers in the world. The portrait was conducted as a creative collaboration between myself and holographers Jeffrey Robb. Robert Munday and Dr John Perry, using a digital stereogram camera specially commissioned for the task and a 3D scanner.

The original hologram was unveiled by Prince Charles at the Jersey Museum in June 2004. The 'lenticule' shown here in the castle was made using the same images that were recorded for that historic hologram.

Neil Mahrer:
Reproduction artillery at Mont Orgueil

The first two cannon you will see on a visit to Mont Orgueil, the swivel gun in the Cornish Bastion and the larger weapon on the Grand Battery, represent the earliest style of iron gun. Until the mid-sixteenth century it was not possible to cast large iron weapons, and they had to be painstakingly built up from smaller pieces of wrought iron. First, long thin staves were made to surround a temporary wooden core and then red hot iron rings were squeezed around them to shrink on cooling, holding the whole barrel tight. Both of these weapons are breechloaders, that is they have a removable back end into which the powder and ball are placed.

Nathan Twomey and other staff of Rylance Ltd, architectural ironworks in St Helier, undertook the ironwork for these two weapons, only the second and third such wrought-iron cannon to be made in the last 450 years. JHT volunteers Mike Blake and James Main carved the wooden carriage for the gun on the Grand Battery from a single elm tree trunk. Although power tools were used at times, the bulk of the work was done in the traditional fashion.

Mike and James also made the medieval catapult on the Grand Battery. This is a type known as a perrier and was operated by three people pulling ropes. Even a small catapult of this type could throw stones weighing several kilograms a considerable distance.

The cannon on the Mount Battery is a reproduction of an early seventeenth-century saker that shot a nine-pound cannon ball. The barrel is on loan from the Royal Armouries and sits on a field carriage designed to be towed by horses. Once again, the JHT volunteers made the carriage. Cast-iron barrels of this type replaced the earlier wrought-iron ones because, being much stronger, they allowed a more powerful and accurate shot to be used.

Steve Manthorp:
Prayer/story nuts

This commission was a rare and welcome opportunity for me to create a substantial body of work. For me, a major commission is often an object that the commissioner can enclose in a single hand, so embarking on a set of twelve elaborate carvings was both an exciting and a daunting prospect. I have a great love of medieval miniature carving, so the prayer nut, the devotional object that wealthy medieval Christians carried to reflect upon, was a natural choice of form.

Perhaps because Jersey has retained its own identity whilst being influenced and fought over by surrounding countries for centuries, it is rich with history and legend. Although all the stories I worked from are associated with Saints Mary and George, the carvings are not devotional, but illustrative. They might be better described as 'story nuts'.

I chose to work in boxwood, which is treasured by carvers because it takes fine detail and retains its strength even when thinly carved or undercut. I designed the nut on computer. The blanks were skilfully turned by Kevin Sanderson. I drew the pattern on each exterior by hand and modelled the interior designs in plasticine from drawings. I did some 'roughing out' with a mini-drill, but most of the carving was done with scalpels and tiny chisels ground from jewellers' screwdrivers. The carvings were smoothed by scraping with a blade and were finished with wax.

Mark Griffin:
Springald

Springalds were fairly numerous but were lightly made, and because they were largely made from organic materials (timber, leather, horsehair rope) they have not survived. Because of this, it has been necessary to go back to the original medieval sources to find descriptions of them and how they worked. When this information was combined with the information taken from various manuscript illustrations, it became possible to recreate the 'war engine'. A particularly impressive image is held in the Bodleian Library in Oxford.

These engines were capable of firing darts with a pointed head or a pot filled with inflammable material. We know from records that Mont Orgueil was stocked with 'sulphur vivum' – living sulphur – as early as 1326; this was probably for use in 'fiery darts', which could be launched by springalds such as this.

Although the springald here in Mont Orgueil will be displayed mounted on top of the Second Gate, it was actually designed and made up like the originals so that it can be taken to pieces and then re-assembled. Because it is housed outside, horsehair rope would disintegrate fairly quickly and so a modern synthetic material has been used instead.

Bill Ming and Stan Bullard:
The Jersey prisoners sculpture

Initially, figurative studies were made in poses that depicted the misery and despair of incarceration, and maquettes were then made from these studies. Life-size figures were carved from lime wood after initially using a chainsaw to bring the large, heavy trunks to an approximate shape and size.

The final stage of the carving involved using different chisel and gouge marks on the surface of the figures to represent the look and feel of clothes, skin, hair, etc.

The sculptures were then given several coats of waterproofing, which soaks into the wood. Danish oil was then applied to help resist damage by rain and a damp atmosphere.

The metal restraints were designed after visits to castles and medieval dungeons in the Midlands and northern England to observe the shackles and chains that had been used in the past to restrain prisoners.

By using basic blacksmithing techniques, the restraints were 'made to measure' for each sculpted prisoner. All restraints had a professional coating of zinc and anti-rust powder to resist the coastal wind and weather.

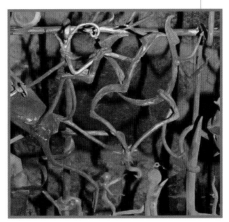

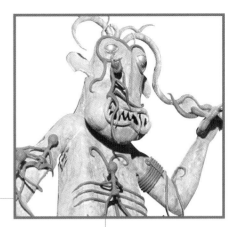

Mike Woods:
The witches

In making this piece I used techniques that would have been familiar to metalworkers in the sixteenth century, as well as modern fabrication methods and 21st-century tools. Before starting the project I delved into various books on medieval witchcraft, featuring artists such as Bosch and Breughel. Many other lesser-known artists, and some who are anonymous or long forgotten, inspired me, and I have incorporated some references to them.

Similarly, there are some references to witchcraft, both local and generic. A Jerseyman, Jean Mourant, sacrificed a finger to his satanic master. I have shown this, along with other witchcraft references, such as a bottle of urine for protection from spells, a dead man's hand for making spells, witches' familiars such as frogs, cats and bats, a witches' sabbat, copulating with the devil, etc.

The abbreviated quote on the grille is by Philippe Le Geyt, 1635-1715, commentator and Lieutenant Bailiff.

Gregg Wagstaff:
Sound design in St George's Crypt
(Long Cellar)

Sounds form a rich and meaningful part of our being, yet history reveals very little about the changing nature of the sounds that ceaselessly envelop our lives.

To help us to 'open our ears' to the castle's past soundscapes, I searched historical documents for references – various artefacts, including a mass book and breviary, served as a starting point for the sound design in St George's Crypt (the Long Cellar). It was the existence (in the Société Jersiaise) of a fourteenth-century manuscript by a monk called John that led me to spend three days with the Benedictine monks of Pluscardine Abbey in Scotland – home to some 23 monks who continue their 'divine office' in Latin. The recordings of bells, Mass and prayer that I made on location at Pluscardine are heard in the crypt. The design (or 'composition') of the sound plays on a spatial narrative, and relates both a personal and collective sense of worship.

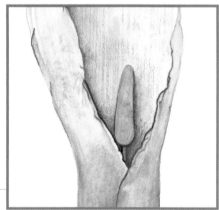

Dixie-Lee Whiteman:
The flora and fauna of Mont Orgueil

The original brief instructed me to produce a number of illustrations, mainly of the castle flora, in a contemporary style, based on a medieval herbal. When I began researching the project, I initially looked at the way in which plants had been depicted at that time.

The illustrations were beautifully, yet very simply, executed. I soon realised that the requirements of this project would mean that, although I also wanted to keep the work I produced very simple, in order for people to use my illustrations as reference material, my work would need to be more detailed.

Consequently, I had a great struggle trying to produce work that was not overly decorative but was easily identifiable.

There was one abiding image to which I kept returning and which helped to keep the project on track, and that was a copy of a page from the 'Great Herbal', from the Abbey of Bury St Edmunds.

The illustrations themselves were produced in watercolour, pencil and ink. I occasionally made use of acrylic and pastels. Although they may look simple, each one was time-consuming. Probably the most difficult part was the research that I had to undertake just to make certain I had identified the correct plant to illustrate.

Gordon Young:
Engraved stones

Whether the material is stone, wood, steel, glass or 'urines', the works take form and have contents which I hope contribute towards a narrative or narratives of the place.

To not necessarily do the obvious does not mean that what is done is not an appropriate thing to be doing; imagination should come into play and is a reason for an artist being used. To create a mental 'trip' and cause a slight wobble to reality is not harmful and can be healthy and rewarding. To engage, charm, shock, puzzle or enlighten, can all contribute to such trips and can gain and hold attention. The actuality of the place, along with the narratives using the newly built, can be a way to nurture interest, respect, knowledge and, ultimately, a love for the place. What adds up to making the place so special and precious? Not all aspects will ever be touched upon by 'interpretation' (nor should it, in my view), but our aim with Mont Orgueil, as creative people, was to face up to the business of what, where, how, why and for whom. The skills, experience and materials used by us to try to make sense of and share aspects of the castle has resulted in a chain of stuff. What stories emerge and what facts amaze, excite or engage, may change. That seems to me normal, as it is the story of a dynamic place and we are just contributing a little early in the twenty-first century.

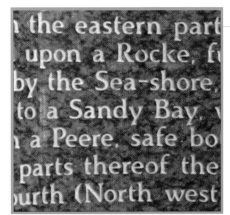

Josh Young:
Inventory of arms and armour

The video illustrates the castle inventory of arms and armour from 1224 to 1583. None of the objects survives as a Jersey example, so the purpose is to show what baldrics, blackbilles, hauberks and quarrels, etc actually are. The piece presents the inventory in chronological order, utilising typography, 3D illustration and compositions that combine footage of re-enactors shot on a blue-screen with photographs taken of Mont Orgueil and the surrounding area. (Re-enactors: Stunt Action. Sound design: Clive Meaker.)

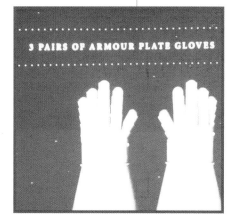

First published Jersey 2007

By the Jersey Heritage Trust
Jersey Museum, The Weighbridge, St Helier,
Jersey, JE2 3NF

ISBN 978-0-9552508-2-8

Acknowledgements

The author would like to thank the following
people for their help, advice and contribution of
material for this souvenir guide: Dr Warwick
Rodwell, Dr Neil Rushton, Professor Colin Platt, and
all his colleagues from the Jersey Heritage Trust
who supported him during its writing, especially
Mel Warrs for his unfailing assistance with proof
reading.

Picture Credits

Photographs supplied by

Stuart Abraham, Robin Briault, Gordon Collas, Doug Ford, Sven Ford,
Cassie Horton, Chris Levine, Nigel Utting

Société Jersiaise Photographic Archive 32

Bundesarchiv 13

British Library 5 & 5

Jersey Heritage Trust / Société Jersiaise Collection 8, 10, 11, 12, 12, 23, 27 & 53

Computer renders by Peter Stewart
Pencil drawings by Richard Bryant
Plans by Warwick Rodwell

Further Information

Balleine, G.R. (1973): The Tragedy of Philippe d'Auvergne
Dixon, P & Kennedy, J (2002): Mont Orgueil Castle Conservation Plan
Everard, J.A. & J.C. Holt (2004): Jersey 1204: The forging of an Island Community
Ford, D (2004): Jersey 1204: A Peculiar Situation
Nicolle, E.T. (1921): Mont Orgueil Castle. Its History and Description.
Platt, C (2001): Mont Orgueil Castle and the Defence of Jersey 1540-1630
Platt, C (2003): The Mont Orgueil Dossier
Rodwell, W.J. (2006) Mont Orgueil Castle, Jersey. History and Architecture
Rybot, N.V.L. (1933 and later editions): Gorey Castle, Jersey

Jersey
Heritage Trust